How to Draw
Maryland's
Sights and Symbols

Jenny Deinard

The Rosen Publishing Group's
PowerKids Press™

Published in 2002 by The Rosen Publishing Group, Inc.
29 East 21st Street, New York, NY 10010

First Edition

Book Design: Kim Sonsky
Layout Design: Nick Scaccia
Project Editors: Jannell Khu, Jennifer Landau

Illustration Credits: Jamie Grecco, except p. 13 by Emily Muschinske.
Photo Credits: p. 7 © Bettmann/CORBIS; p. 8 © Bill Schmidt (sketch), © Bill Schmidt (photo); p. 9 © Bill Schmidt; pp. 12, 14 © One Mile Up Incorporated; pp. 16, 18 © Index Stock; p. 20 © D. Robert & Lorri Franz/CORBIS; p. 22 © Photo courtesy of USS Constellation Museum; p. 24 © William A. Bake/CORBIS; p. 26 © (B & O Train Station) David H. Wells/CORBIS, (Steam Locomotive) Colin Garratt; Milepost 92½ /CORBIS; p. 28 © Kevin Fleming/CORBIS.

Deinard, Jenny
        How to draw Maryland's sights and symbols /
Jenny Deinard.
          p. cm. — (A kid's guide to drawing America)
        Includes index.
        Summary: This book explains how to draw some of Maryland's sights and symbols, including the state seal, the official flower, and the Baltimore oriole, the official state bird.
        ISBN 0-8239-6076-5
        1. Emblems, State—Maryland—Juvenile literature 2. Maryland—In art—Juvenile literature
3. Drawing—Technique—Juvenile literature   [1. Emblems, State—Maryland   2. Maryland
3. Drawing—Technique]   I. Title   II. Series
        2001
        743'.8'99752—dc21

Manufactured in the United States of America

CONTENTS

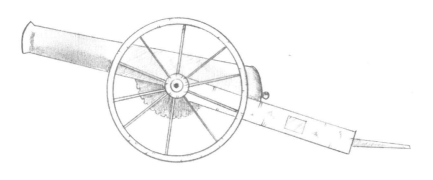

Let's Draw Maryland

Maryland was the seventh state to join the Union, on April 28, 1788. It has a varied landscape, with coastal plains, valleys, farmlands, and mountains. Waterways play a large role in Maryland. In fact 16 of the 23 counties in Maryland border water. The Chesapeake Bay, which divides the state into eastern and western Maryland, was one of the country's most important waterways in the eighteenth century. Today many people in Maryland make their living by catching seafood in the bay. The port of Baltimore is one of the busiest ports in the United States. The Potomac River, upon whose banks Washington, D.C., is built, also passes through Maryland.

Maryland is also a state rich in history. Important battles were fought on Maryland's soil during the Revolutionary War, the War of 1812, and the Civil War. Francis Scott Key wrote "The Star-Spangled Banner" after he saw British troops attack Fort McHenry in Baltimore during the War of 1812. The Treaty of Paris, which ended the Revolutionary War, was signed in the city of Annapolis in 1784.

You can use this book to learn more about Maryland's history and how to draw its sights and symbols. Each drawing begins with a simple shape. From there you will add other shapes. Directions under the drawings explain how to do the steps. New steps are shown in red to guide you. To draw Maryland's sights and symbols, you will need:

- A sketch pad
- An eraser
- A number 2 pencil
- A pencil sharpener

These are some of the shapes and drawing terms you need to know to draw Maryland's sights and symbols:

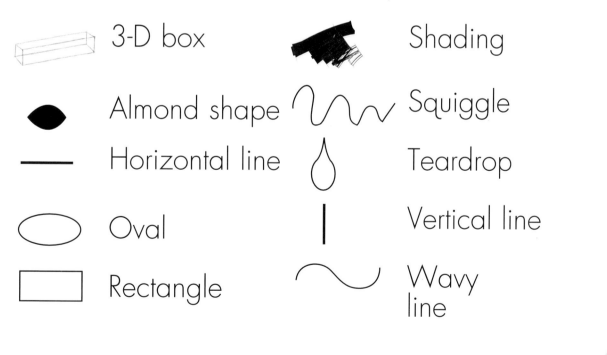

3-D box

Shading

Almond shape

Squiggle

Horizontal line

Teardrop

Oval

Vertical line

Rectangle

Wavy line

The Old Line State

Maryland began as an English colony. King Charles I named Maryland after his wife, Queen Henrietta Maria. In 1632, the king granted the charter for Maryland to George Calvert, the first Lord Baltimore. Calvert died before the charter was completed. His son Cecilius, the second Lord Baltimore, received the charter and sent settlers to the colony in 1634. Today Baltimore is the largest city in Maryland, with 675,400 residents. Maryland has more than 5 million residents, and covers 12,297 square miles (31,849 sq km) of land.

Maryland is often called the Old Line State. This name came from George Washington, who praised the bravery of Maryland's "troops of the line" during the Revolutionary War. Maryland also is called the Free State. Hamilton Owens, an editor of the *Baltimore Sun* newspaper, created the nickname in 1923. He called Maryland the Free State because it did not pass Prohibition, a U.S. law from 1919 to 1933 that made drinking alcohol illegal.

This undated illustration shows the first Lord Baltimore, George Calvert (1580–1632). He wanted Maryland to be a place of religious freedom.

Artist in Maryland

Bill Schmidt

Bill Schmidt is one of Maryland's best-known painters. He is a plein air painter. Plein air is a French phrase that means "open air." It refers to when an artist paints outdoors rather than in a studio. Schmidt paints in the impressionist style. Impressionism began in France in 1867, when early impressionist painters focused on the light, colors, and textures of the outside world. Impressionists such as Monet and Pissarro painted outdoors, letting their paintings show the changes of light that they saw while they painted. Bill Schmidt follows in this tradition, painting countrysides, street scenes, and the marine scenes of Chesapeake Bay.

Before Bill Schmidt painted *Dock Area*, he made sketches to plan it. This is one of his sketches.

Schmidt was born on March 18, 1932, in Bayonne, New Jersey. Schmidt had a successful career as an engineer, but he also loved to paint landscapes. He spent many weekends painting and studying art with landscape painters. Schmidt moved to Maryland in 1967, and, in 1984, he started painting full-time. Schmidt has shown his work in America and in Japan. Two of Schmidt's paintings hang in the American Embassy in Sarajevo, Bosnia.

This painting, entitled *Dock Area*, shows a view of Annapolis from the city's dock. The painting measures 18" x 24" (46 cm x 61 cm).

Map of Maryland

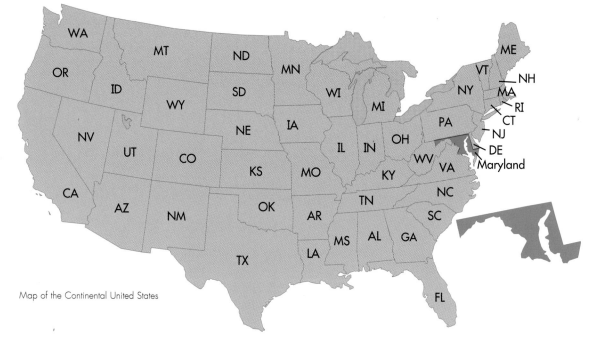

Map of the Continental United States

Maryland borders Delaware, Pennsylvania, West Virginia, Virginia, and the District of Columbia. Maryland's northern border is called the Mason-Dixon Line. The border was named after Jeremiah Dixon and Charles Mason, two famous surveyors. Although Maryland has no natural lakes within its borders, 23 rivers run through the state. Maryland is also home to the Chesapeake Bay, the East Coast's largest estuary. The bay nearly cuts the state in half! The word "chesapeake" comes from a Native American word that means "great shellfish bay." Maryland's highest point is Backbone Mountain, located in the western corner of the state. Backbone Mountain rises 3,360 feet (1,024 m) above sea level.

1

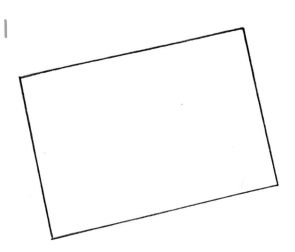

Start by drawing a slanted rectangle.

2

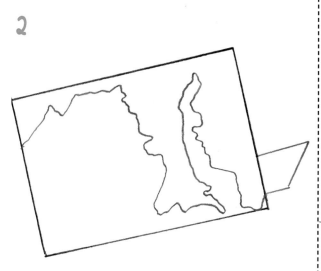

Using the rectangle as a guide, draw the shape of Maryland as shown.

3

Erase extra lines.

☆ Annapolis

◯ Assateague Island National Seashore

☐ Baltimore

✕ Antietam National Battlefield

⌂ Clara Barton's house

4

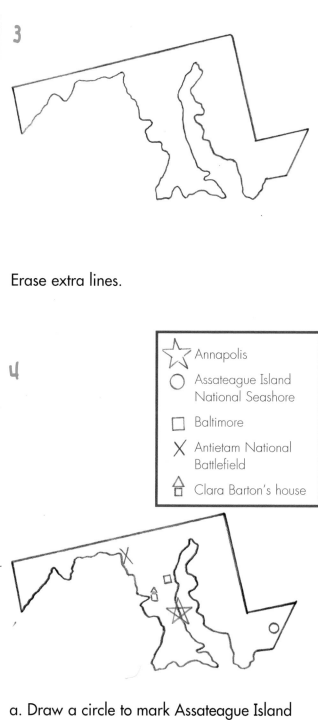

a. Draw a circle to mark Assateague Island National Seashore.
b. Draw in a square to mark Baltimore.
c. Use an X to mark Antietam National Battlefield.
d. Use a square and a small triangle to mark Clara Barton's house.
e. Draw a star to mark Annapolis, the capital of Maryland.

The State Seal

Maryland's first great seal came from England after the colony was settled in the 1600s. The seal was changed over the years. In 1876, Maryland adopted a seal much like the first one. The seal has two sides. The front shows an image of Lord Baltimore, the colony's founder. He wears armor and rides a horse that is draped in a cloth showing the Baltimore family coat of arms. The back of the seal, the side that most people see, shows a farmer and a fisherman holding a shield of the Baltimores' coat of arms. One of the state mottoes, Manly Deeds, Womanly Words, appears on the banner at the bottom. The date on the seal, 1632, is the year Maryland received its charter.

front

back

1

Begin by drawing a shield.

2

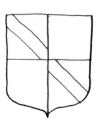

Divide it into four parts. Add diagonal lines as shown.

3

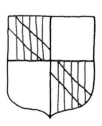

Add vertical lines.

4

Add two plus symbols as shown, using one vertical line and one horizontal line for each. Then create a rounded cross on top of each plus symbol using four *U* shapes as shown.

5

Draw a crown on top of the shield.

6

Add the shape of a person's shoulders, neck, and head. Put a crown on top of the head.

7

Draw the banner and print the state motto on it. Add a cross to the top of the crown.

8

Add shading and detail.

13

The State Flag

The state flag of Maryland bears the coats of arms of the Calvert and the Crossland families. The Lords Baltimore who founded the colony of Maryland were Calverts. The first Lord Baltimore's mother's family name was Crossland. The flag is divided into four quarters. The first and fourth quarters are made up of six vertical bars in gold and black, the Calvert family colors. The second and third quarters are red and white, the colors of the Crossland family. These two quarters are shaped like the Greek cross. The flag was first flown on October 11, 1880, at a celebration for the150th anniversary of the founding of the city of Baltimore. The flag was made official in 1904, 116 years after Maryland became a state.

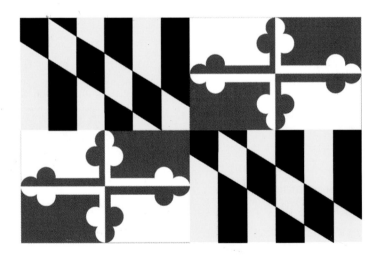

1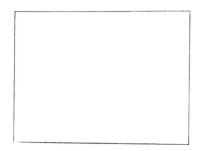

Start by drawing a large rectangle for the flag's field.

2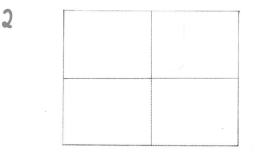

Next divide the flag into four parts.

3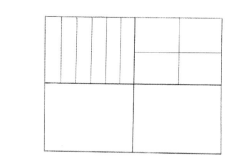

Draw five lines in the upper left box and divide the upper right box into four parts.

4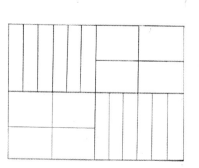

Next divide the lower left box into four parts and draw five lines in the lower right box.

5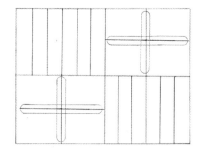

Add two long ovals to the top right and lower left boxes.

6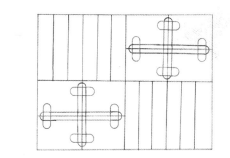

Make a small oval on the end of each long oval.

7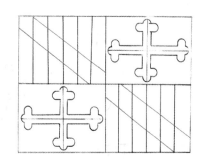

Erase extra lines and add two diagonal lines across the upper left and lower right boxes.

8

Erase any extra lines and smudges, and shade in the flag.

The Black-Eyed Susan

In 1896, at a meeting at the Maryland Agricultural College, a group of women decided that Maryland should have a state flower. The group chose the black-eyed Susan, a common wildflower in Maryland. Twenty years later, in 1918, the black-eyed Susan was adopted officially as the state flower of Maryland. One of the reasons that the black-eyed Susan was chosen for Maryland was that it is black and gold, which are colors in the Maryland flag. Black-eyed Susans, part of the sunflower family, have either dark brown or black centers and have golden yellow petals. They grow throughout most of North America, although one variety of the flower is native to Maryland.

1

Start by drawing a circle for the center of the flower.

2

Then add about 14 small triangles around the circle.

3

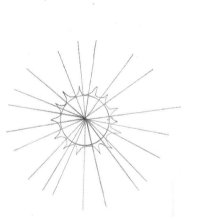

Draw about 20 lines from the center of the circle. These lines will mark where each petal goes.

4

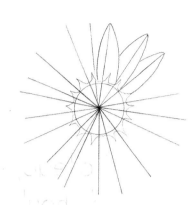

Draw curved lines for the petals.

5

Finish drawing the petals, and erase extra lines.

6

Add shading and detail to your flower, and you're done.

The White Oak

In 1941, Maryland adopted the white oak (*Quercus alba*) as its state tree. The largest white oak in the United States lives in Maryland at Wye Mills on the eastern shore. This tree, called the Wye Oak, is more than 100 feet (30.5 m) tall and is more than 400 years old! White oaks have whitish gray bark and shiny leaves with a handlike shape. The leaves fall off in winter.

Oak trees begin to grow acorns when they are about 50 years old. They can grow more than 10,000 acorns every year! Native Americans taught early Maryland settlers to grind acorns into flour.

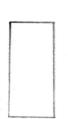

1

Start by drawing a long rectangle for the tree's trunk.

2

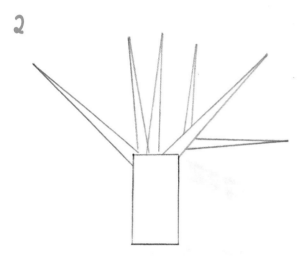

Next add about six triangles over the rectangle for branches.

3

Draw thinner branches using wavy lines. Use the rectangle and triangles as guides to add wavy and rounded lines so the branches and tree trunk look more natural.

4

Use any shapes you like to add snow on the tree. Erase any extra lines.

5

Add shading and detail, and you're done. Make the snow a lot lighter than the tree bark.

The Baltimore Oriole

The Baltimore oriole (*Icterus galbula*) became Maryland's state bird in 1947. According to one story, Lord Baltimore admired the birds' black-and-gold coloring, which was like the colors in his own coat of arms. "Baltimore birds" were sent to England in 1698, to show the British an example of Maryland wildlife. In 1758, the famous naturalist Linnaeus named the species the Baltimore oriole, after Lord Baltimore. The male has a black head, back, and chest, and an orange tail and underbelly. His wings are black with white tips. The female has an olive-colored head and back with black spots, and yellowish olive tail feathers. Her wings are dark with white tips, and her underbelly is yellow-orange.

1

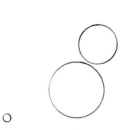

Start by drawing three circles for the oriole's head and body.

2

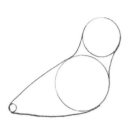

Connect the circles to form the oriole's body.

3

Erase any extra lines.

4

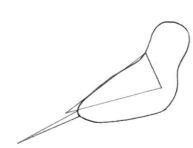

Draw two triangles, one for the tail and one for the wing.

5

Use two triangles to draw the oriole's beak.

6

Use two triangles for the top of the oriole's legs and add an eye. Add detail to the beak and round the outline of the wing.

7

Use thin lines to draw the feet. Draw part of a rectangle and curved lines for a tree stump.

8

To finish your oriole, erase extra lines and add detail and shading. You can use your finger to smudge the pencil lines.

21

The USS Constellation

The USS *Constellation* is a ship with a mysterious past. In 1797, the U.S. Navy launched a frigate warship named *Constellation* from Baltimore, Maryland. A frigate carries guns on one deck. In 1955, an old ship that had been rotting in Boston Harbor was moved to Baltimore. People believed this was the 1797 *Constellation*. In 1991, the ship was proved to be an 1854 sloop of war, also named the *Constellation*. A sloop of war carries all her guns on one deck. This

Constellation is the last all-sail ship built by the U.S. Navy, and it was used during the Civil War. Today the restored *Constellation* sits in Baltimore's Inner Harbor. Visitors come each year to see the last Civil War ship in existence today.

1

Begin with a rectangle. This will be your guide as you draw the shape of the ship's hull. The hull is the lower part of the boat that sits in the water.

2

Erase extra lines. Add horizontal lines to divide the ship into sections. Notice how the front of the ship is taller than the back and comes to a point. This helps the ship break through the waves as it moves through the high seas.

3

Add two small circles for portholes, or windows, in the boat's hull. Add two curved lines for the rope that hangs on the side of the boat. Add slanted lines for the detail on the hull.

4

Add a tall triangle with a line down the middle to the front of the ship.

5

Add three tall masts. These are the poles that hold the sails. Add three oval platforms to each mast.

6

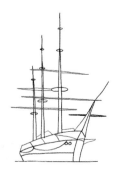

Next add crossbars to the masts and add rigging, or equipment, to the hull.

7

The next part is tricky. Draw a lot of ropes that stretch from the mast to different areas of the ship. These ropes help the crew control the sails. Add the flag on the front of the ship.

8

Add shading and detail. You're done!

23

Antietam National Battlefield

Antietam National Battlefield in Sharpsburg, Maryland, is the site of the Civil War's bloodiest battle. More than 23,000 men were killed or wounded when General Robert E. Lee's Confederate army fought Major General George B. McClellan's Union army on September 17, 1862. The battle at Burnside Bridge, then known as Rohrbach Bridge, was the third and final part of the battle. Major General Ambrose Burnside led Union troops across the stone bridge to fight the Confederate troops on the other side. Although neither side won at Antietam, it was a victory for the Union troops in that they succeeded in stopping General Lee's invasion of the Northern states.

1

Start by drawing one large circle with a smaller circle inside for the wheel of the cannon.

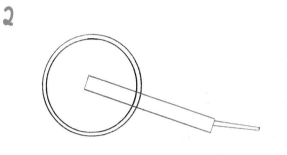

2

Then add a rectangle and a triangle for the cannon's brace, or leg.

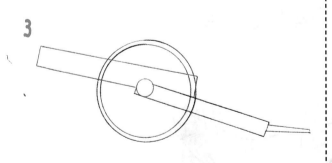

3

Add another small circle in the center of the wheel and a rectangle for the shape of the cannon. Erase extra lines.

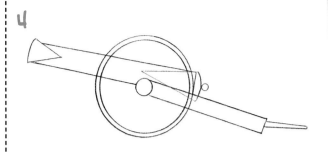

4

Add a triangle with rounded ends to each end of the cannon and a small circle at the rear.

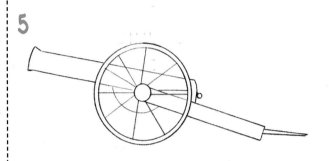

5

Erase extra lines. Add a half circle to the bottom of the cannon and spokes in the wheel.

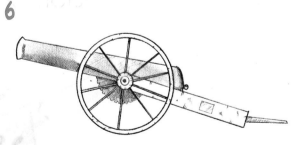

6

Add shading and detail, and you're done.

Baltimore and Ohio Railroad Station

Ellicot City, once called Ellicot Mills, is home to America's first railroad terminal, the Baltimore and Ohio Railroad Station. The two-story station, finished in 1831, is the country's only remaining nineteenth-century railroad station. In 1856, passenger waiting rooms and a telegraph and ticket office were built on the second floor of the station. Passenger service continued until 1949. The Baltimore and Ohio Railroad Station was named a national historic place in November 1968. Today it serves as a museum, offering a living history of America's early transportation and travel industries. A 50-foot (15-m) turntable, used to turn railroad cars around, and a caboose from 1927 are on display.

1

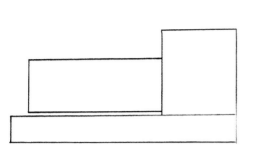

Start by drawing three rectangles as shown.

2

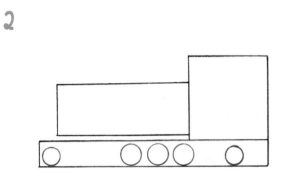

Add five circles for wheels. The front and rear circles are smaller.

3

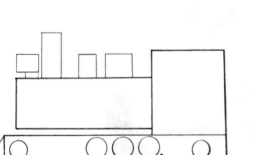

Draw five more small rectangles on top of the engine as shown and a triangle in the front.

4

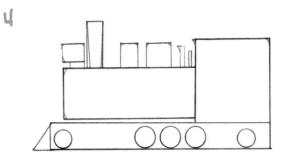

Add two more, thin rectangles and round off the edges of all of the rectangles.

5

Erase extra lines. Add four more rectangles.

6

Add shading and detail, and you're done. You can also add smoke and steam rising from the train.

27

Maryland's Capitol

Maryland's capitol building, called the Maryland State House, is the oldest capitol in the country that is still in use. It is the only capitol to have served as the United States's capitol building, from 1783 to 1784. The original architect was Joseph Horatio Anderson. Construction began on March 28, 1772, but was slowed down by hurricanes and the American Revolution. The capitol took more than seven years to finish. In 1785, architect Joseph Clark repaired the leaking roof. Clark added a wooden dome topped with a lightning rod that was based on the designs of Benjamin Franklin. The rod is connected to the dome by a 5-foot-tall (1.5-m-tall) acorn made of cypress wood. The capitol is a national historic landmark.

1

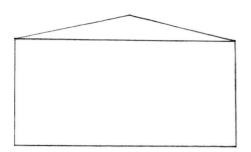

Start by drawing a large rectangle with a triangle above it.

2

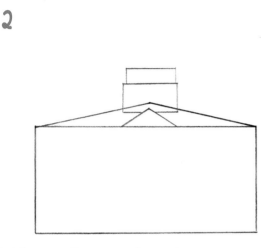

Add a smaller triangle and two small rectangles.

3

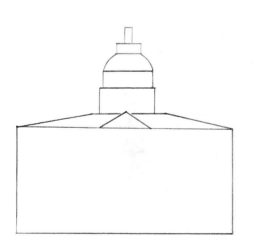

Erase extra lines. Add a half circle and two small rectangles for the dome.

4

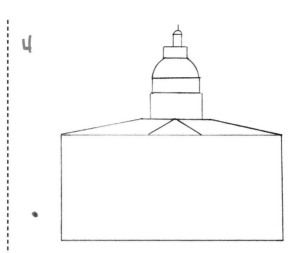

Add another half circle and a short, straight line for the peak of the dome.

5

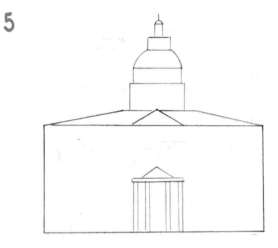

Add a small triangle and five thin rectangles for the front entryway.

6

Use rectangles for the windows. Add shading and detail to your building. Erase any extra smudges, and you're done.

29

Maryland State Facts

Statehood	April 28, 1788, 7th state
Area	12,297 square miles (31,849 sq km)
Population	5,171,600
Capital	Annapolis, population, 33,200
Most Populated City	Baltimore, population, 675,400
Industries	Real estate, health services, business services, engineering services, communications, banking, insurance
Agriculture	Dairy products, poultry and eggs, nursery stock, soybeans, corn, seafood, cattle
Tree	White oak
Song	"Maryland! My Maryland!"
Bird	Baltimore oriole
Flower	Black-eyed Susan
Fossil Shell	*Ecphora gardnerae gardnerae* (extinct snail)
Dog	Chesapeake Bay retriever
Boat	Skipjack
Fish	Striped bass
Crustacean	Maryland blue crab
Insect	Baltimore checkerspot butterfly
Sport	Jousting

Glossary

adopted (uh-DOPT-ed) To have accepted or approved something.

charter (CHAR-tur) A written document that allows an area to be used but not owned.

Civil War (SIH-vul WOR) The war fought between the northern and southern states of America from 1861 to 1865.

coat of arms (KOHT UV ARMZ) A design on and around a shield or on a drawing of a shield.

Confederate (kuhn-FEH-duh-ret) Relating to the group of people who made up the Confederate States of America.

embassy (EM-buh-see) The official home and office in a foreign country of a government official and his or her staff.

estuary (ES-choo-wehr-ee) An area of water where the tide meets a river.

frigate (FRIH-git) A three-masted sailing ship that carries its guns on a single gun deck.

industries (IN-dus-treez) Systems of work, or labor.

landmark (LAND-mark) An important building, structure, or place.

marine (muh-REEN) Having to do with the sea.

naturalist (NACH-er-uh-list) A person who specializes in the study of things in nature.

Revolutionary War (reh-vuh-LOO-shuh-ner-ee WOR) The war between the colonies and Britain that resulted in the United States becoming its own country.

sloop of war (SLOOP UV WOR) A sailing ship rigged with guns for war.

surveyors (ser-VAY-erz) People who study the land.

telegraph (TEH-lih-graf) A machine used to communicate through coded signals.

War of 1812 (WOR UV AY-teen TWELV) A war between the United States and Britain, fought from 1812 to 1815.

Index

Web Sites

To learn more about Maryland, check out this Web site: www.state.md.us